究竟是谁干的?

Who Did It?

[美]威力·布莱文斯/著　　[美]吉姆·帕约/绘

王婧/译

电子工业出版社

Publishing House of Electronics Industry

北京·BEIJING

本书中文简体版专有出版权由Red Chair Press LLC通过CA-Link International LLC授予电子工业出版社，未经许可，不得以任何方式复制或抄袭本书的任何部分。

版权贸易合同登记号　图字：01-2022-0735

图书在版编目（CIP）数据

究竟是谁干的？ / (美) 威力·布莱文斯 (Wiley Blevins) 著；(美) 吉姆·帕约 (Jim Paillot) 绘；王婧译. -- 北京：电子工业出版社，2023.6
（胖狗和瘦狗）
ISBN 978-7-121-44941-3

Ⅰ. ①究… Ⅱ. ①威… ②吉… ③王… Ⅲ. ①儿童故事－图画故事－美国－现代 Ⅳ. ①I712.85

中国国家版本馆CIP数据核字(2023)第077361号

责任编辑：范丽鹏
印　　刷：天津图文方嘉印刷有限公司
装　　订：天津图文方嘉印刷有限公司
出版发行：电子工业出版社
　　　　　北京市海淀区万寿路173信箱　邮编：100036
开　　本：787×1092　1/16　印张：26.25　字数：264千字
版　　次：2023年6月第1版
印　　次：2023年6月第1次印刷
定　　价：208.00元(全8册)

凡所购买电子工业出版社图书有缺损问题，请向购买书店调换。若书店售缺，请与本社发行部联系，联系及邮购电话：(010) 88254888，88258888。
质量投诉请发邮件至zlts@phei.com.cn，盗版侵权举报请发邮件至dbqq@phei.com.cn。
本书咨询联系方式：(010) 88254161 转 1862，fanlp@phei.com.cn。

目录

闪亮登场的主角们

艾克

克鲁德

绒球小姐

鲍勃

马丁太太

有人在敲门！

砰砰砰！砰砰砰！砰砰砰！

"是谁在敲门呀？"艾克问。

"快来呀，鲍勃，"克鲁德汪汪大叫，"快去开门！"

"也许是有人带来了美味的食物呢。"艾克舔了舔嘴巴说。

"是马丁太太。"克鲁德说。

"她的脸怎么了?"艾克问。

"她满脸通红而且很不高兴的样子。"克鲁德汪汪大叫着,"快跑!"

他们飞快地朝桌子底下冲去。克鲁德的鼻子露在了外面,而艾克的尾巴露在了外面。

"克鲁德和艾克在哪里?"马丁太太凶巴巴地喊。

"呃哦……"克鲁德小声嘟囔。

"有人偷了我家绒球小甜心的玩具老鼠。她之前在围栏那儿玩得好好的，结果玩具没了，不见了，被偷了。她现在可伤心了，都不肯再对我'喵'一下了。"马丁太太说。

　　"哦，太令人伤心了。"鲍勃说。紧接着他打了个响指，喊道："快出来，小伙子们，就现在！"

克鲁德和艾克摇摇晃晃地蹭到了鲍勃的脚边。但是他俩谁都没有抬头看一眼鲍勃。

"小伙子们，你们俩有没有拿走不属于自己的东西？"鲍勃问。

克鲁德立马摇了摇头，但他的尾巴却指向了艾克。而艾克摇了摇自己的尾巴，但他的爪子却指向了克鲁德。

鲍勃蹲下来看着他俩，说："既然如此，那你们其中的一个得去把丢失的东西找回来，不然的话……"

"'不然的话'是什么意思啊？"艾克小声问。

"就是鲍勃不知道自己要说什么话的时候说的话。"克鲁德说，"总之，就是大事不妙的意思。"

鲍勃转身对马丁太太说："如果东西在这儿的话，我们一定会找到的。"

"那就这样吧。"马丁太太说完怒气冲冲地走了。

6

　　"你把绒球小姐的玩具藏到哪儿去了？"克鲁德问。

　　"我根本没拿过啊。"艾克说，"你拿过吗？"

　　"当然没有啦！"克鲁德说，"她一直把那个玩具叼在嘴里，**恶心**死了！"

　　"所以，我们现在该做点什么呢？"艾克问。

　　"我们最好找到那个玩具。"克鲁德回答。

　　"可是怎么找呢？"艾克问。

"如果那东西在这里的话，我们的鼻子一定会先知道的。"克鲁德说。

"对呀，"艾克说，"那咱们就用尽一切办法去寻找吧！可是我们要从哪里开始找起呢？"

"从鲍勃的房间开始怎么样？"克鲁德说。

"可是那里什么都没有啊。"艾克说。

"没错，但是那里有很多地方适合躲藏呀！"克鲁德说，"准备好了吗？"

"我都听你的，哥们儿！"艾克说。

他们跑进了鲍勃的房间。克鲁德拉开抽屉，艾克跳了进去，他把里面的东西全都给刨了出来——什么有洞的袜子啦，扯坏的T恤啦，还有穿旧的绿色和粉色的内裤。

"那个玩具不在这儿。"艾克说。

"是的。"克鲁德说，"但是鲍勃真的需要买些新衣服了。"

"那现在怎么办？"艾克问。

"我们去床上看看。"克鲁德说。

克鲁德把枕头扔了下去，然后钻到被子底下，汪汪大叫起来："这儿什么也没有！"隔着被子的克鲁德发出低沉的隆隆声。

艾克抬头就看到床上一个巨大的隆起的鼓包。"啊——有一只巨大的臭虫！"他大叫一声冲到了床底下。

克鲁德摇摇晃晃地走到床边，结果叽里咕噜地滚了下去，大头朝下跌在地上。

"啊——"艾克冲着克鲁德大头朝下的脑袋大叫了起来。

"是我啊，哥们儿！"克鲁德说。

"嘿！"艾克喊道，"瞧瞧我发现了什么，是狗狗零食！"

"所以，这里其实是鲍勃藏零食的地方！"克鲁德说着弄翻了装零食的盒子，然后大口大口地啃起狗骨头来。

"待在这下面可真是太舒服啦！"艾克说。

"是呀，"克鲁德说道，"我都想打个盹儿了！"

"好呀，"艾克说，"反正我们也没什么其他更好的事情可做。"于是这两个家伙蜷缩着躲在床底下，没过多一会儿就打起了呼噜。

　　"这里究竟……发生了……什么呀！"鲍勃气得大吼。克鲁德和艾克吓得立马蹿了起来。

　　"噢！"克鲁德一下磕到了脑袋，疼得他汪汪直叫。"哎哟！"艾克也跟着大叫起来。

　　"快出来！现在！立刻！马上！"鲍勃命令道，"不然的话……"

　　"呃哦……"克鲁德小声嘟囔。

　　"他刚才又说了那句'不然的话'。"艾克小声说。

　　这时，鲍勃抓住了他们，将他们从床底下拽了出来。

　　"出去！出去！出去！"鲍勃指着门口大声说，"快走！"

"鲍勃为什么要把我们轰出来呢？"艾克问。

"或许他现在想让我们到院子里去搜查一下吧。"克鲁德说。

忽然，一道小小的身影出现在了他们的头顶上方。

克鲁德和艾克慢悠悠地抬头一看。

"哦，艾克。"克鲁德说。

"哦，克鲁德。"艾克说。

绒球小姐趴在围栏上，她慢慢地、长长地叹了一口气："**喵，哦，天呀！**"

　　"你瞧，"艾克说，"她伤心得甚至都不想像舔棒棒糖似的舔自己的爪子了。"

　　"得了吧，"克鲁德说，"我可不想整天看着她垂头丧气的样子，咱们还是继续走吧。"

　　绒球小姐来回甩着尾巴，然后慢慢地又长长地叹了一口气："**喵，哦，**这是为什么呀！"

克鲁德开始在草地上闻了起来。"嘿，哥们儿，"他突然汪汪大叫，"我想我有新发现了。"

"对不起。"艾克说。

"不，我是说这是很好闻的味道。"克鲁德说，"跟我来。"

他们一边走一边闻，闻啊闻啊闻，爬上院子的高坡，再爬下院子的高坡，按照"之"字形路线向前寻找着。

"嘿！"艾克突然叫起来，"让我想一想啊。"

"怎么了？"克鲁德问。

"我想我发现了点什么，"艾克说，"这是什么？"

克鲁德靠近看了看，使劲闻了闻，结果打了个喷嚏。于是他又舔了舔地上的一小块灰色的痕迹。"太有趣了，"克鲁德说，"我想你刚刚发现了我们的第一条线索。"

"什么线索？"艾克问。

"可以带我们找到丢失的玩具老鼠的线索。"克鲁德说。

"什么丢失的玩具？"艾克问。

"绒球小姐的玩具老鼠啊。"克鲁德说。

"哦，对呀，我们得找到那个东西，"艾克说，"对吧？"

"当然了，"克鲁德说道，"所以我们剩下的时间不多了，快来吧！"

"我们跑这么快要去哪啊？"艾克问。

"跟着地上这条灰色毛球留下来的痕迹走。"克鲁德说。

"为什么呀？"艾克问。

"因为这些灰色的毛球就是绒球小姐玩具的一部分，跟上去就能找到我们要找的东西，并且抓住那个窃贼。"

19

“抓住窃贼？”艾克脚下一个“急刹车”停了下来，“我可不想遇到什么窃贼！况且，我们遇到了这个被你称为‘窃贼’的家伙以后，该怎么办？我这么小可不能遇到窃贼啊，我这么漂亮更不能遇到窃贼了，而且，而且，而且我对鲍勃来说太重要了！”

　　“等我们穿过那条小路到那里的时候，”克鲁德说道，“就是破案的时候啦！”克鲁德正说着，突然扭过头，问道：“你看到我看到的东西了吗？”

　　“一棵树吗？”艾克问。

　　“不是。”克鲁德说。

　　“还是你尾巴上的跳蚤？”艾克反问。

　　“不是。”克鲁德说。

　　“难道是问你的屁股有多大吗？”艾克问。

　　“**当然**不是啦！”克鲁德指了指院子的角落。

21

　　"汪汪嗷！"克鲁德大叫起来。"汪汪哦！"艾克大喊起来。鲍勃和马丁太太听到了他们的叫声，跑到后院来。连绒球小姐也顺着围栏悄悄地靠了过来。

　　"哦，我的，天啊！"马丁太太惊呼，"竟然有一
窝兔子宝宝！"

　　"是呀，"鲍勃说，"一定是兔子妈妈把绒球小姐
的玩具老鼠拽到这里的，看看裹在兔子宝宝身边的那些
东西。"

绒球小姐开始哈气，然后很大声地 "哼" 了一下，朝着屋子飞快地跑了回去。

"看来，我需要给她买个新玩具了。"马丁太太说。然后她转身对克鲁德和艾克说："谢谢你们发现了这些，我想这功劳属于你们中的一个。"

"我认为应该是艾克。"克鲁德汪汪叫道，然后用他的尾巴指向了艾克。

"我认为应该是克鲁德。"艾克汪汪叫道，然后用他的爪子指向了克鲁德。

他们默契地撞了下彼此的屁股，然后开心地朝家跑去。

"先别急，小伙子们。"鲍勃指着院子的另一边说道。

　　"看来我们又惹祸了。"克鲁德说。

　　"这没什么大不了的,"艾克说,"反正鲍勃的房间需要好好地打扫一下了,我可不想在乱糟糟的地方睡觉!"

　　"我也是。"克鲁德说。

于是，艾克和克鲁德摇摇晃晃地朝着狗窝走去。他们彼此依偎在一起，进入了长长的并且鼾声不断的香甜梦乡。可他们怎么又打起盹儿来了呢？好吧，这应该就是与最好的朋友携手破案之后，该做的事情吧！

Meet the Characters

Ick

Crud

Miss Puffy

Bob

Mrs. Martin

The Knock

KNOCK! KNOCK! KNOCK!

"Who is pounding on the door?" asked Ick.

"Come on, Bob," barked Crud. "Open that door."

"Maybe it's someone bringing yummy treats," said Ick.

And he licked his lips.

有人在敲门!

砰砰砰! 砰砰砰! 砰砰砰!

"是谁在敲门呀?" 艾克问。

"快来呀, 鲍勃," 克鲁德汪汪大叫, "快去开门!"

"也许是有人带来了美味的食物呢。" 艾克舔了舔嘴巴说。

1

"It's just Mrs. Martin," said Crud.

"What's wrong with her face?" asked Ick.

"It's all scrunchy and red."

"RUN!" barked Crud.

The two dashed under a table. Crud poked out his nose. Ick poked out his tail.

"Where are Ick and Crud?" shouted Mrs. Martin.

"Uh-oh," whispered Crud.

"Someone stole a toy mouse from my sweet Miss Puffy. She was playing with it by the fence. And now it's gone, gone, gone! She's so upset she can barely *meow*."

"Oh, no," said Bob. Then he snapped his fingers. "Come on out, boys, now."

Ick and Crud waddled to Bob's feet. But neither could look at him.

"Boys, did one of you take something that doesn't belong to you?"

Crud shook his head. But his tail pointed to Ick. Ick shook his tail. But his paw pointed to Crud.

Bob squatted to look them in the face. "Well, one of you needs to find it. OR ELSE!"

2

The Search

"What does 'OR ELSE' mean?" whispered Ick.

"It's what Bob says when he can't think of something to say," said Crud. "And it's not good."

Bob turned to Mrs. Martin. "If it's here, we'll find it."

"I should think so," said Mrs. Martin. And she left in a huff.

"Where did you hide Miss Puffy's toy?" asked Crud.

"I didn't take it," said Ick. "Didn't you take it?"

"Of course not," said Crud. "She put it in her mouth. *Ewww!*"

"So, what do we do?" asked Ick.

"We better find it," said Crud.

"How?" asked Ick.

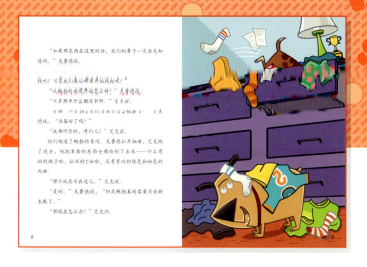

"If it's here, our nose will know," said Crud.

"Yes," said Ick. "Let's leave no stone unturned. Where do we begin looking?"

"How about Bob's room?" said Crud.

"There are no stones in there," said Ick.

"No, but there are lots of hiding places," said Crud. "Are you ready?"

"I will if you will, buddy," said Ick.

The two raced into Bob's room. Crud pulled open drawers. Ick jumped in and kicked out whatever he found inside. Socks with holes. Shirts with rips. Old green and pink underpants.

"No cat toys here," said Ick.

"No," said Crud. "But Bob really needs some new clothes."

"Now what?" asked Ick.

"Let's look on the bed," said Crud.

Crud tossed off the pillows. Then he slipped under the covers. "Nothing here," he barked. But it sounded like a low rumble.

Ick looked up and saw the big bump on the bed. "AAAAAGH! A giant bedbug!" he screamed and darted under the bed.

Crud wiggled to the end. Then rolled off. He landed upside-down on the floor.

"AAAAAGH!" yelled Ick as he looked out at Crud's upside-down face.

"It's only me, buddy," said Crud.

"Hey," said Ick. "Look what I found. Dog treats!"

"So this is where he hides them," said Crud. He tipped over a box and chomped on a big bone.

"It's so cozy down here," said Ick.

"这里究竟……发生了……什么呀！"鲍勃气得十着肩膀伸和甘多吓嚷口，高强了姓身
"啾！"克鲁德一下墙到了脑袋，疼得他汪汪直叫。"哎哟！"艾克也跟着大叫起来。
"快出来！现在！立刻！马上！"鲍勃命令道，"不然的话……"
"呃哦……"克鲁德小声嘟囔。
"他刚才又说了那句'不然的话'。"艾克小声说。
这时，鲍勃抓住了他们，将他们从床底下拽了出来。
"出去！出去！出去！"鲍勃指着门口大声说，"快走！"

"Yes," said Crud. "I think it's time for a nap."

"Okay," said Ick. "We have nothing better to do." The two snuggled under the bed. And soon they were snoring.

"WHAT…HAPPENED…HERE?!" shouted Bob. Crud and Ick shot up.

"Ow-wee," barked Crud as he bumped his head. "Eee-ow," yelped Ick.

"Get out here now," said Bob. "OR ELSE!"

"Uh-oh," whispered Crud.

"He said 'OR ELSE' again," whispered Ick.

Just then Bob grabbed the two and slid them from under the bed.

"Outside, outside, outside!" he said. Bob pointed to the door. "Go!"

The Clue

"Why did Bob send us outside?" asked Ick.

"Maybe he wants us to search in the yard now," said Crud.

Just then a small shadow moved above them.

Crud and Ick slowly looked up.

"Oh, ick," said Crud.

"Oh, crud," said Ick.

Miss Puffy slumped on the fence. She let out a long, slow sigh: *meow-oh-my*.

"Look," said Ick. "She's so sad she can't even lick her paws like they're lollipops."

"Well," said Crud. "I can't look at her droopy face all day. Let's keep going."

Miss Puffy flicked her tail back and forth. Then she let out another long, slow sigh. *Meow-oh-why*.

Crud began sniffing the grass. "Hey buddy," he barked. "I think I smell something."

"Sorry," said Ick.

"No, this is a good smell," said Crud. "Follow me."

The two went sniff, sniff, sniffing. Up the yard. Down the yard. And in a zig-zag.

"Hey," said Ick. "Stop the doggie door."

"What?" asked Crud.

"I think I found something," said Ick. "What is this?"

　　克鲁德靠近看了看，使劲闻了闻，结果打了个喷嚏。于是他又舔了舔地上的一小块灰色的痕迹。"太有趣了，"克鲁德说，"我想你刚刚发现了我们的第一条线索。"

　　"什么线索？"艾克问。

　　"可以带我们找到丢失的玩具老鼠的线索。"克鲁德说。

　　"什么丢失的玩具？"艾克问。

　　"绒球小姐的玩具老鼠啊。"克鲁德说。

　　"哦，对呀，我们得找到那个东西，"艾克说，"对吧？"

　　"当然了，"克鲁德说道，"所以我们剩下的时间不多了，快来吧！"

18

Crud looked closer. He took in a deep sniff and sneezed. Then he licked the little piece of gray. "Very interesting," he said. "I think you found our first clue."

"Clue to what?" asked Ick.

"A clue to find the missing toy," said Crud.

"What missing toy?" asked Ick.

"Miss Puffy's toy mouse," said Crud.

"Oh right, we need to find that," said Ick. "Don't we?"

"Yes," said Crud. "And we don't have much time. Hurry!"

Success?

"Where are we going so fast?" asked Ick.

"Follow the path of gray fuzz," said Crud.

"Why?" asked Ick.

"Each gray fuzz ball is a piece of Miss Puffy's toy. These pieces will lead us to it. And to the thief!"

成功破案了吗？

"我们跑这么快要去哪啊？"艾克问。
"跟着地上这条灰色毛球留下来的痕迹走。"克鲁德说。
"为什么呀？"艾克问。
"因为这些灰色的毛球就是琺琲小姐玩具的一部分，跟上去就能找到我们要找的东西，并且抓住那个窃贼。"

19

"The thief?" asked Ick. He skidded to a stop. "I don't want to meet a thief! What will we do when we find this thing you call a thief? I'm too young to meet a thief. I'm too pretty to meet a thief. I'm…I'm…I'm too important to Bob."

"We'll cross that doggie path when we get there," said Crud. "It's time to solve the crime." Crud quickly twisted his head. "Do you see what I see?"

"A tree?" asked Ick.

"No," said Crud.

"That flea on your tail?" asked Ick.

"No," said Crud.

"How big your butt is getting?" asked Ick.

"*Really* no," said Crud. Then he pointed to the corner of the yard.

"汪汪噢！" 克鲁德大叫起来。"汪汪噢！" 艾克大喊来。鲍勃和马丁太太听到了他们的叫声，跑到后院来。连绒球小姐也顺着围栏悄悄地靠了过来。

"哦，我的，天啊！" 马丁太太惊呼，"竟然有一窝兔子宝宝！"

"是呀，" 鲍勃说，"一定是兔子妈妈把绒球小姐的玩具老鼠拖到这里的，看看裹在兔子宝宝身边的那些东西。"

22

23

"*Ruff. Ruff. Grrr*," barked Crud. "*Ruff. Ruff. Cough*," yelped Ick. Bob and Mrs. Martin heard the noise. They raced to the back of the yard. Miss Puffy slinked closer on the fence.

"Oh, me-oh-my," yelled Mrs. Martin. "It's a nest of baby rabbits."

"Yes," said Bob. "The mother rabbit must have dragged Miss Puffy's toy mouse here. Look at how the baby rabbits are snuggled around it."

毛球小姐开始哈哈气，然后很大声地"咔"了一下，朝着屋子飞快地跑了回去。

"看来，我需要给她买个新玩具了。"马丁太太说。然后她转身对克鲁德和艾克说："谢谢你们发现了这些，我想这功劳属于你们中的一个。"

"我认为应该是艾克。"克鲁德汪汪叫道，然后用他的尾巴指向了艾克。

"我认为应该是克鲁德。"艾克汪汪叫道，然后用他的爪子指向了克鲁德。

他们默契地撞了下彼此的屁股，然后开心地朝家跑去。

Miss Puffy let out a hiss and a loud *ACK!* Then she shot off toward the house.

"I guess I'll need to get her a new toy," said Mrs. Martin. She turned to Ick and Crud. "Thank you for finding this. I was sure one of you had taken it."

"I thought it was Ick," barked Crud. And he pointed his tail to Ick.

"I thought it was Crud," barked Ick. And he pointed his paw to Crud.

Then the two butt-bumped and headed back to the house.

"Not so fast, boys," said Bob. He pointed to the far side of the yard.

"Looks like we're in the doghouse again," said Crud.

"That's okay," said Ick. "Bob has a lot of cleaning to do in his room. I don't want to sleep in that big mess."

"Me neither," said Crud.

于是，艾克和克鲁德摇摇晃晃地朝着狗窝走去。他们彼此依偎在一起，进入了长长的并且鼾声不断的香甜梦乡。可他们怎么又打起盹儿来了呢？好吧，这应该就是与最好的朋友携手破案之后，该做的事情吧！

28

So, the two waddled to the doghouse. There they snuggled and took another long, snore-filled nap. Why? Because that's what best friends do after solving a crime.